KILLING THE BEAR

Jonathan Yukich

BROADWAY PLAY PUBLISHING INC
New York
www.broadwayplaypublishing.com
info@broadwayplaypublishing.com

KILLING THE BEAR
© Copyright 2020 Jonathan Yukich

Cover art: Mark Minnig

First edition: April 2020
I S B N: 978-0-88145-862-6

Book design: Marie Donovan
Page make-up: Adobe InDesign
Typeface: Palatino

KILLING THE BEAR, under its previous title BALLS, was first presented as part of New York University's hotINK International Festival of Play Readings in January of 2010. The cast and creative contributor were:

MARY MERLE .... Maggi Low
POSEY ....Doug Paulson
KEEGAN .... Eric Clem
RUTHIE... Rachel Simpson
BRODY ....Stephen Tyrone Williams

Director ....Jim Abar

CHARACTERS & SETTING

MARY MERLE MOON, *early forties*
POSEY MOON, *a high school senior*
KEEGAN MOON, *a high school senior*
RUTHIE, *a high school senior*
BRODY, *late forties*

Time: 1974

The home of the MOON *family. Southern, lower middle class. A living room and kitchen, no wall dividing. Up center, a modest stairway and front door. In the living room, a sliding door leading to the backyard. On the walls of the home are mounted, antique firearms and two framed pictures: one of Jesus Christ, the other of Bear Bryant.*

ACT ONE
Scene 1: Thursday Morning
Scene 2: Thursday Night

ACT TWO
Scene 1: Friday Morning
Scene 2: Friday Night

You shall know the truth, and the truth shall make you odd.
Flannery O'Connor

ACT ONE

(At rise:)

(The MOON *family home. Empty, dark, late. Faint slithers of moonlight trickle through the windows. Silence. Stillness)*

(In the night, a sound. Gradually, a ferocious engine-like rumbling from without, descending above the house, closer and gaining intensity. Items rattle as intense, probing lights beam through every orifice of the home, shining through from the ceiling, turning the interior, momentarily, into a flash of stunning brightness. Afterward, the rumbles and beams steadily fade away. Stillness again. Fade to black)

Scene One

(Thursday morning)

(Lights up full on MARY MERLE MOON, *exuberant and cheerful. She wears her morning robe and cooks bacon at the stove.)*

MARY MERLE: I declare, boys, it's a beautiful mornin' in Balls! Come down and eatcha some breakfast! Mama's fixin' her bacon! Ain't it the best? Mama makes it good like! Same ways daddy useta! There's a right way of doing it! Takes touch and flair, yes sir—good bacon does. Takes class! *(Begins to set a place at the table)* Oh, it's a grand day in Balls! Just wait till you hear why. Come on now—get your pig! You two ain't never

been on time. Even during your birthin'. It was like
you didn't want to come out. Matter of fact, you two
near kilt me. Here you come, all tangled together, like
you was yoked. Doctor even thought so, that you was
conjoined. 'Least for a second. Thought you was one
of them bonded ruinations you see on the T V, the way
you was clingin' to each other. Stubborn little poots.
I wonder, what were you two doing in there? In the
womb, I mean, to make you come out such as you was.
Life's here just waitin' to meet ya—and the two of you
pop out a twisted heap of flesh, with four eyes so wide
and alive youda thought you'd seen eternity!

(POSEY *has appeared, fully dressed, holding a book, and
staring at his mother from the bottom of the stairs.*)

POSEY: Did you see'em?

MARY MERLE: *(Startled)* Oh—Posey. Is Keegan up?

POSEY: Did you see'em?

MARY MERLE: See who, dear?

POSEY: The aliens.

MARY MERLE: The who's-it?

POSEY: They were right on top the house.

MARY MERLE: Probly that possum.

POSEY: Their lights was flashing in.

MARY MERLE: Scuzzy possums.

POSEY: You had to of seen'em.

MARY MERLE: I sleep so heavy, Posey dear, nothin' stirs
me. You read too many books, bright boy. Makes you
behave extremely. What's that one you got there?

POSEY: *Crime and Punishment* by Dostoyevsky.

MARY MERLE: See now. What good's it do you to be
readin' some German?

POSEY: Russian.

MARY MERLE: Help me Jesus.

POSEY: These aliens, they're gettin' closer each visit.

MARY MERLE: That's enough now.

POSEY: Soon they're gunna be in our livin' room.

MARY MERLE: Hush it.

POSEY: How could you not have seen'em?

MARY MERLE: Nowhere in the Scripture, Posey, is there mention of little green men. So there ain't none. If there was, the Lord woulda said so. I'm sure of it. Besides, even if they was real, what would aliens want with Alabama? With Balls? With this house, this family?

POSEY: That's what I'm aimin' to figure.

MARY MERLE: Huntin' spooks—that's what you're doin', bright boy.

POSEY: What's that smell?

MARY MERLE: Bacon.

POSEY: Bacon?

MARY MERLE: *(A big smile returns.)* I made bacon.

POSEY: Oh my lord. Why would you go do a thing like that?

MARY MERLE: A new dawn has broke in Balls.

POSEY: There ain't been bacon in this house since daddy died.

MARY MERLE: There's a magic about.

POSEY: Whole house smells of smoke.

MARY MERLE: You seen the mornin' paper, bright boy?

POSEY: Not sure I wanna.

MARY MERLE: It's sittin' on the sofa. Front page. Go 'head, take a gander.

POSEY: I can't imagine what'd bring about bacon.

MARY MERLE: Go on. Right yonder.

POSEY: I think I'd rather not to.

MARY MERLE: Uh-uh-uh! You gotta! Here! *(Takes the paper and thrusts it in his face)* Whatcha make of this, bright boy?

POSEY: *(Reading)* "Two-Headed Cow Dazzles County Fair."

MARY MERLE: No! The photo! Up top!

POSEY: Oh my lord.

MARY MERLE: Ain't that the berries?

POSEY: Oh my lord.

MARY MERLE: What'd I tell ya, bright boy? A new dawn!

POSEY: That's Keegan!

MARY MERLE: Ain't he handsome in his uniform? Looky at the headline.

POSEY: "Coach Paul Bear Bryant to Visit Balls." You're jokin' me.

MARY MERLE: To Balls, Posey. Bear Bryant's comin' to Balls!

POSEY: Who's Bear Bryant?

MARY MERLE: Don't tell me you don't know who Bear Bryant is. He's only the most famous football coach alive.

POSEY: Why's he comin' here?

MARY MERLE: *(With reverence)* To recruit Keegan to play football at the University of Alabama.

POSEY: He gunna give'im a scholarship?

MARY MERLE: If he likes what he sees, and I predict he will.

POSEY: But Keegan's just a punter.

MARY MERLE: So?

POSEY: Bear Bryant's gunna come to Balls to see a punter? I didn't think they give punters scholarships.

MARY MERLE: What the hell you know 'bout football? Everybody needs'um a punter. Even the mighty Crimson Tide. Keeg can kick'em fifty-five yards on average. That ain't usual, Posey. Boy's got T N T in his toes!

POSEY: But how'd they find him in Balls?

MARY MERLE: Coach Tutt.

POSEY: But Coach Tutt's just the high school coach.

MARY MERLE: He knows people at the university— that's where he studied P E. He made a phone call and they sent someone secret to scout him last week. Musta liked what they seen. So now the Bear's comin' down personal. Tomorrow night!

POSEY: Can't be.

MARY MERLE: Oh, it be. Coach Paul Bear Bryant, in the flesh. It's 'bout the biggest news in Balls since Mayor Dudley got caught in that whorehouse down in Dothan.

POSEY: This is too much.

MARY MERLE: A blessin' is what it is.

POSEY: *(Visibly shaken)* It's warm in here.

MARY MERLE: Naw.

POSEY: Blood's rushin' in my head. I got galloping in my head.

MARY MERLE: You alright, bright boy?

POSEY: I'm not, no.

MARY MERLE: You need the Pepto?

POSEY: Beg pardon, mama.

MARY MERLE: Pardon for what?

POSEY: For this. (*He closes his eyes tight and clinches his fists to his side, belting an agitated, prolonged screech.*)

MARY MERLE: Lord Awmight!

(POSEY *continues to belt, part grunt, part shriek. Roused by the shrieking, dogs are heard barking from outside.*)

MARY MERLE: Posey! The hell's got into you!

POSEY: This is how I escape my nightmares, mama.

MARY MERLE: Nightmares—?

POSEY: I holler so loud I wake the dreamin' part of myself up.

(POSEY *returns to his outburst.* MARY MERLE *slaps him across the face.*)

POSEY: Mama! What'd you do that for?

MARY MERLE: You was screamin' like a stuck pig! Listen them dogs out there! You gunna get us thrown out of this town!

POSEY: I was nearly waked up.

MARY MERLE: You been waked, boy. Why can't you be proud of your brother? Why's this family's good fortune gotta be tied to a nightmare?

POSEY: There's just one place set at the table.

MARY MERLE: Only Keegan gets bacon. You get Cocoa Puffs.

POSEY: He gets the world and I get Cocoa Puffs—all on account he can kick a ball.

MARY MERLE: We all got that one special thing.

POSEY: What's mine, mama?

(Pause. No answer.)

POSEY: Mama?

MARY MERLE: I'm thinkin'.

POSEY: This is what I mean. We got not means for measuring real value in this town. There's a great wide world out there, but nobody sees beyond their own noses!

MARY MERLE: Don't start with them aliens again.

POSEY: I think, last night, they landed.

MARY MERLE: Good. Maybe they'll take you back with'em.

POSEY: I reckon I'd do anything to get outta Balls.

MARY MERLE: Better loosen them britches, Mr Big. There's plenty of great wide world right here in Balls, if you'd bother to stop readin' them Soviets and notice.

KEEGAN: *(From off, upstairs)* What's all the holler down there?

MARY MERLE: *(Beaming with anticipation)* He's awake! Keegan's awake, Posey!

POSEY: I'll get the rose petals…

(KEEGAN *slumbers down the stairs, groggy and nearly naked, wearing only his briefs and an ankle weight around one of his ankles. He walks with supreme confidence, cock of the walk, and no trace of inhibition.* POSEY *moves to the kitchen table, sits brooding.)*

KEEGAN: Sounds like Bull Run 'tween these walls.

MARY MERLE: Mornin', baby boy.

KEEGAN: Why's Big Dog and Patty Cake actin' a fit?

MARY MERLE: Your brother had him a conniption.

KEEGAN: Another one?

MARY MERLE: His brain's inflamed.

KEEGAN: I smell cookin'.

MARY MERLE: Keegan, dear, you got any idea the miracle mornin' we find ourselves in?

KEEGAN: Smells like bacon.

MARY MERLE: Just for you.

KEEGAN: Bacon for me?

MARY MERLE: Yep.

KEEGAN: Let's have at it.

MARY MERLE: Don't you wanna know 'bout the miracle?

KEEGAN: While I eat.

MARY MERLE: Before you do, honey, feast your eyes here! Sha-zam!

(MARY MERLE *flashes the front page before* KEEGAN.)

KEEGAN: *(Reading)* "Two-headed Cow Dazzles County Fair." Yeah I heard 'bout that.

MARY MERLE: No, no. Up top.

KEEGAN: Well, hot dang. That's me in my pads.

MARY MERLE: Dignified, aint'cha?

KEEGAN: *(Snatching the newspaper from her.)* "Coach Paul Bear Bryant to Visit Balls."

MARY MERLE: To see you play football!

KEEGAN: Me?

MARY MERLE: He wants to watch you punt.

KEEGAN: Against Ridge Valley? Tomorrow night?

MARY MERLE: Sure 'nough.

KEEGAN: This a joke?

MARY MERLE: 'Course not. Hand to God, baby boy.

KEEGAN: I brought the Bear to Balls? Oh, mama!

MARY MERLE: Ain't it magical, honey?

(KEEGAN and MARY MERLE embrace. Then KEEGAN paces, pumped with adrenaline.)

KEEGAN: Wooo-hooo! Hot dang it! Look at that, wouldja! I been recognized!

MARY MERLE: By the Bear, no less.

KEEGAN: (Admiring, almost dreamily, Bryant's picture on the wall.) The greatest coach ever, comin' to see me personal. He must be interested in me playin' football for him—for the Alabama Crimson Tide. He must be thinkin' of given me one of them scholarships!

MARY MERLE: Must be.

POSEY: Score one for Einstein.

KEEGAN: What'd you say?

MARY MERLE: Must be.

KEEGAN: No—Posey. What'd Posey say?

MARY MERLE: What'd you say, Posey?

POSEY: I dunno.

KEEGAN: You was makin' small of me.

POSEY: I was?

KEEGAN: You was.

MARY MERLE: What'd you say, Posey?

POSEY: I said Brothers Forever.

KEEGAN: Liar! He said "Score one for Einstein", as if to say I ain't Einstein.

POSEY: You ain't?

MARY MERLE: Posey's very witty.

KEEGAN: You seen the newspaper?

POSEY: Got my own copy pinned above my bed.

KEEGAN: Oh, you're a real hardy-har. Look atcha. Why you gotta be so queer?

POSEY: I ain't the one with a bracelet on my foot.

KEEGAN: *(Bristling)* It ain't a bracelet! It's an ankle weight! I wear it so I'm workin' my guns even when I'm snoozin'!

MARY MERLE: Always betterin' hisself. That's just the sort a' scruples the Bear's after.

POSEY: All this state cares about is football—the oracle of the South! And what are you worshipping, mama, really? Young boys ramming each other over a piece of hog hide. What's more queer than that?

MARY MERLE: Don't slur the game, Posey. We done lost the war, had our way of life literally burned to ash. But football we're good at. Any team—north, south, east, west—that's stepped in front the Crimson Tide has gotten crushed to the earth.

POSEY: 'Cept for Notre Dame.

MARY MERLE: *(Sharply)* I told you never mention the Catholics in this house.

KEEGAN: You know your problem, Posey? All the thinkin' you do, you ain't ever had a thought that mattered.

POSEY: Mattered to you, maybe.

KEEGAN: Mattered to anybody! People 'round here can't even believe we come outta the same womb. They're outright embarrassed for me—havin' to put up with a fat-headed brother spoutin' crap nobody cares about!

POSEY: Better a fat-head than a butt-face.

KEEGAN: Shut up.

POSEY: You shut up.

KEEGAN: Fruit.

POSEY: Ingrate.

KEEGAN: Chump.

POSEY: Mongoloid.

KEEGAN: Nelly.

POSEY: Thief.

(MARY MERLE *gasps. Silence. The word "thief" has sucked the air from the room.*)

MARY MERLE: Posey! Not that word! Never that word! What's Keeg ever stole?

POSEY: He knows.

MARY MERLE: Keeg, what've you stole?

KEEGAN: I never stole nothin', mama, you know that. He's just jealous.

POSEY: You both know of what I'm speakin'. Let's get it in the open.

KEEGAN: I'm 'bout to open your face with my knuckles.

POSEY: Why're you afraid?

KEEGAN: I ain't afaid! Mama, I cain't concentrate on puntin' with his ribbin' at me.

MARY MERLE: (*Taking a seat on the sofa*) No more about this! You leave him quiet, Keegan, and come sit next to me.

KEEGAN: This house don't respect me none!

MARY MERLE: Keegan, obey your mama.

KEEGAN: That chump's gunna get what's comin' to him!

MARY MERLE: (*Firmly*) Com'ere, I said, and park it.

(KEEGAN *obeys, sitting beside* MARY MERLE *on the living room sofa. She takes him in her arms, putting his head on her shoulder and stroking his hair as she speaks.* POSEY *returns to the kitchen.*)

MARY MERLE: Listen now: this game tomorrow evenin', this is your occasion with destiny, Keegan. A chance to lift this family and all of Balls from its knees. You can't let nothin' stand in the way of that.

KEEGAN: He just burns me up.

MARY MERLE: Cage that energy and use it for good.

KEEGAN: The game.

MARY MERLE: The game, baby boy.

KEEGAN: You think daddy'd be proud?

MARY MERLE: I think he'd give up heaven to be here.

KEEGAN: I wish he could see me punt.

MARY MERLE: He's lookin' down, most sure. His own son, playing for the Crimson Tide. It's what every daddy in Alabama dreams of. His done come true…

KEEGAN: Mama, what if I drop the ball?

MARY MERLE: Don't talk like that.

KEEGAN: What if I freeze up?

MARY MERLE: You ain't froze before.

KEEGAN: But Bear Bryant ain't been watchin' me before neither. Everybody's countin' on me. What if I let'em down?

MARY MERLE: Failure ain't in ya, honey. Like the Book says: "A city set on a hill cannot be hid." Your daddy and I knew that from the crib. A blessin' come to us in baby form. You're our city on a hill.

(POSEY *scoffs quietly, irritated by the syrupy talk. Spitefully, he moves to the stove and stealthily begins to cram his mouth with the bacon.*)

MARY MERLE: Don't matter what life throwed in front of you, you'd rise above. It's somethin' divine, somethin' rooted deep within.

KEEGAN: Am I bona fide special, mama?

MARY MERLE: Bona fide. A spit-image of your daddy. Both of you could take life by the neck and punch it right 'tween the eyes.

KEEGAN: That's what I'm figurin' to do tomorrow night—punch life 'tween the eyes.

MARY MERLE: More like kick it 'tween the eyes.

(KEEGAN *and* MARY MERLE *laugh.* POSEY *smiles mockingly, unnoticed, cheeks bloated with bacon.* MARY MERLE'S *laugh turns weepy.*)

KEEGAN: You aight, mama?

MARY MERLE: I'm proud as a peach of you, boy.

KEEGAN: You're gettin' soggy on me.

MARY MERLE: Pay me no mind, precious. Eat your bacon. I made it special for you. It's on the—

(KEEGAN *and* MARY MERLE *look toward the stove, finding* POSEY *staring back at them, mouth full of bacon.*)

MARY MERLE: Posey, your head's swelled up!

KEEGAN: My bacon! He done ate my bacon!

MARY MERLE: I declare! He has!

KEEGAN: I'll kill'im! I'm gunna rip out his guts!

(KEEGAN *starts at him.* POSEY *shields himself behind the kitchen table. They circle,* KEEGAN *on the prowl,* POSEY *on guard.*)

MARY MERLE: Boys!

KEEGAN: We's 'bout to take a trip to Fist City, bright boy! No use tryin' to juke me! Com'ere! That bacon was mine!

(POSEY *begins to pull chunks of bacon from his mouth and throw them at* KEEGAN.)

KEEGAN: Oh, keep on! Just keep on!

MARY MERLE: Posey Moon! Stop hurlin' bacon in this house!

KEEGAN: I'm gunna lump you up!

MARY MERLE: I ain't Hooverin' that rug, Posey! You are!

KEEGAN: Wait till I get hold of'im! I'll make him scarf it up with his teeth!

(*There's a knocking at the front door. Everyone freezes. Silence.*)

MARY MERLE: Reckon who that could be?

(MARY MERLE *answers the door. It's* RUTHIE, *a sprightly redhead wearing an oversized Balls High letterman's jacket and smacking gum.*)

RUTHIE: Mornin', Mother Moon. How y'all today?

MARY MERLE: *(Flatly)* Fine, Ruthie. It's Ruthie everybody.

RUTHIE: *(Making her way inside)* I just seen the *Balls Gazette* and near had a hissy! Where's my hunk?

KEEGAN: *(Coldly staring down his brother)* Hey, babe.

RUTHIE: There he is, the boy who made Balls flutter. What's the matter?

MARY MERLE: There's been some family drama, Ruthie.

RUTHIE: You can tell me. I'm over here so much I feel as if I'm related.

KEEGAN: Posey ate my bacon.

RUTHIE: *(Mock outrage)* Barbarian!

KEEGAN: Lucky I ain't kilt him yet. He done poked the tiger!

RUTHIE: Oh stop.

KEEGAN: I'm serious.

RUTHIE: Temper, temper. Relax, would ya? *(She slinks under* KEEGAN's *arm, cozying up.)* Keegan Moon, you gunna pay me some attention?

MARY MERLE: You best put a shirt on with company present.

RUTHIE: Don't bother me none, him not having a shirt.

MARY MERLE: Ruthie, there's self-respect in not being a whore.

RUTHIE: I ain't a whore, Mother Moon—just wise to the world.

MARY MERLE: Keegan, scoot up them stairs and put some clothes on. Posey, feed Big Dog and Patty Cake. High time you boys be gettin' to school.

POSEY: But I fed'um yesterday. It's Keegan's turn.

MARY MERLE: I'm tired of your lip, Posey! Feed them dogs their breakfast!

KEEGAN: Wait for me, babe?

RUTHIE: If it takes forever.

(Angrily, POSEY *exits through the sliding door, slamming it closed, as* KEEGAN *lunges up the stairs, leaving* RUTHIE *and* MARY MERLE *alone together.)*

RUTHIE: You must be so proud, Mother Moon.

MARY MERLE: I done told you to not call me Mother Moon.

RUTHIE: Jeez-Louise. You sure have. It's just what I'm used to.

MARY MERLE: Mrs. Moon will do.

RUTHIE: Did you see the sky last night?

MARY MERLE: Lord have mercy, no I did not.

RUTHIE: There was a brilliant flash of light. Woke me up. Ran to the window, and the sky was a color I'd never seen before. I felt I was witnessing a phenomenon.

MARY MERLE: Mmm.

RUTHIE: Mrs. Moon, why don't you like me?

MARY MERLE: You're a snake with lipstick.

RUTHIE: I'm a dyin' breed. Didja know that?

MARY MERLE: Jezebels don't die off, child. Every generation's got its share.

RUTHIE: I'm talkin' 'bout redheads. By the year 2090, we're s'posed to be extinct.

MARY MERLE: Does me no good in 1974.

RUTHIE: The gene for redheads, it's gunna die out, they say.

MARY MERLE: Says who?

RUTHIE: Scientists. I read it myself, just last week—in the *National Geographic*.

MARY MERLE: Am I supposed to care?

RUTHIE: Countdown's on for us carrot tops. I'm a relic. A livin' antique, I am.

MARY MERLE: That's nice.

(The phone rings in the kitchen.)

MARY MERLE: Don't go messin' things up for my boy, you hear me? He's got the biggest game of his life tomorrow night and doesn't need to be distracted by your—*ways. (Picks up phone, turns sugary sweet)* Hello? Moon residence? Yes'm, this is Mary Merle Moon.

Why, yes sir, I did place the ad. Spare room, good size. Uh-huh, it is. Thirty-five dollars a month, with utilities. Yes sir, I'm home. These days I hardly leave. *(Laughs affably)* This instant? Why, 'course you can. Yes sir, I'll be here. Sure 'nough, bye now. *(Hangs up; glowing)* Well now, I gotta get dressed. I look an outright mess.

RUTHIE: Who was that?

MARY MERLE: Mind yourself, child.

RUTHIE: Sounded like a boarder. You takin' on a boarder?

MARY MERLE: Matter of fact, Nancy Drew, I am.

RUTHIE: You needin' extra money, Mother Moon? You in debt?

MARY MERLE: Not at all.

RUTHIE: Then why take on a renter?

MARY MERLE: I'm lookin' to get the collection cleaned.

RUTHIE: You mean, all the pistols on the wall?

MARY MERLE: They ain't pistols, girl, they're rifles and revolvers. One of the finest antique gun collections in the region. Belonged to Mr Moon and his daddy before him. One day I'll pass'em on to my boys.

RUTHIE: Keegan won't say how Papa Moon died.

MARY MERLE: It weren't pleasant.

RUTHIE: Whole town knows.

MARY MERLE: Good for them.

RUTHIE: They say Papa Moon got soused after Bama lost the '72 Orange Bowl. Went out to the barn—

MARY MERLE: That's enough.

RUTHIE: Posey was the one that found him, wasn't he?

MARY MERLE: This collection meant the world to Forney. Our twentieth anniversary woulda been next year and I thought it fittin' to have his treasures looked to. Got an estimate from Birmingham. It ain't cheap—takes a good penny to hav'em cleaned safe and proper.

RUTHIE: How much all these worth?

MARY MERLE: More than your head. This one here—an original 1860 Colt .44, an officer's revolver—cost Forney a month's wages, but he had to have it. Was the last he purchased. Ain't it fine?

RUTHIE: Yes mam, it is.

MARY MERLE: Thing 'bout all these guns, not a one of'em been fired.

RUTHIE: They ain't been shot?

MARY MERLE: Not a one. Not a single bullet traveled through any these barrels.

RUTHIE: What a waste.

MARY MERLE: That's what Posey says. But, to me, it's what makes them shine. It's comforting to be surrounded by them. All waiting their turn, so full of promise.

RUTHIE: Keegan know 'bout the boarder?

MARY MERLE: He knows I been lookin' the last several months. I'll say somethin' when he comes down. The man sounded right fine over the phone—like an upstandin', official type. Good breedin', you can always tell. I'm gunna fix my face, Ruthie, and put somethin' welcoming on. Don't let Keegan leave without saying bye.

RUTHIE: Yes mam.

(MARY MERLE *exits up the stairs.* RUTHIE *paces around, smacking gum, surveying. She picks up the newspaper. A moment passes.* POSEY *enters through the sliding door, seems a little unsure with* RUTHIE *present. She looks up at him, then back at the newspaper.)*

RUTHIE: It's a good picture.

POSEY: It's alright.

RUTHIE: I's talking about the cow. *(She rises, moves to* POSEY, *stands before him.)* He sure gets you riled up, don't he?

POSEY: It ain't right.

RUTHIE: We'll make it right.

POSEY: How you figure?

*(*RUTHIE *gently kisses* POSEY *on the lips.)*

RUTHIE: Trust me.

POSEY: I don't like seeing you with Keegan.

RUTHIE: It's just a pageant.

POSEY: It rips me up inside.

RUTHIE: It's only for a while longer. He's gunna be our ticket.

POSEY: He's a buffoon.

RUTHIE: *(Flipping through the Dostoyevsky)* This yours?

POSEY: What do you think?

RUTHIE: It's thick. Reading it for school?

POSEY: Not exactly.

RUTHIE: For fun? Aw, that's cute. What's it about?

POSEY: Sin and suffering.

RUTHIE: Sounds like a hoot.

POSEY: To escape poverty, the main character murders his landlady and her sister.

RUTHIE: Does he get away with it?

POSEY: Kinda.

RUTHIE: You believe murders like that really happen?

POSEY: All the time.

RUTHIE: You think?

POSEY: I know. Sometimes murder's the only way to get out from under somethin'.

RUTHIE: Even in Balls?

POSEY: I reckon. What're you getting' at?

RUTHIE: I was thinking maybe we oughta kill Bear Bryant.

POSEY: Ha ha. That ain't funny.

RUTHIE: Wasn't meant to be. *(Pause. She glares purposefully.)*

POSEY: You're serious?

RUTHIE: In these parts, it'd be bigger than Caesar.

POSEY: What's Bear Bryant want with us?

RUTHIE: You're asking the wrong question. It's what we want with him. Bear Bryant's one of the most powerful men in the South. More famous than the governor even.

POSEY: So we kill him?

RUTHIE: Assassinate.

POSEY: Oh come on, Ruthie.

RUTHIE: Remember that movie I was telling you about?

POSEY: You see too many movies.

RUTHIE: The artsy one I saw over in Montgomery, when I was visitin' my cousins.

POSEY: *Badlands.*

RUTHIE: Yeah. About them teens who get in trouble with the law and have to kill their way out of it. Fame fell in their laps. It was their opening, a way to say to the world: I was here, and I left my mark! We'd be in every newspaper in America. Everybody would know our names. Like those teens.

POSEY: That was a movie.

RUTHIE: Based on real people, I heard.

POSEY: You've lost your mind.

RUTHIE: We don't belong here. In Balls. Neither of us.

POSEY: You've thought about this?

RUTHIE: All mornin'. Bear Bryant—he'll visit Keegan after the game. It's polite to make an in-home visit. We'll all be here, sitting around, stiff and formal. Sweet teas. Pecan pie. Then you come up behind him and— blammo.

POSEY: Me? Shoot Bear Bryant? I can't—what would I use?

(RUTHIE *looks to the Colt .44 on the wall.*)

POSEY: One of daddy's guns? No way.

RUTHIE: I can get money. My daddy's shoebox. He don't trust banks. We could run for it. Live on the lam.

POSEY: Not my daddy's guns. He idolized Bear Bryant.

RUTHIE: All your speechifying is just smack, is that it? About this place suffocating you. I'm aimin' to do something about it—or else I'd wash away, like all the other Mother Moons!

POSEY: Those guns, they never been fired.

RUTHIE: It's time.

POSEY: But he's just a football coach. He seems nice.

RUTHIE: His legend will live forever. So will ours.

POSEY: This is over the line.

RUTHIE: You've fallen for me, Posey Moon. No denying it. I ask myself, what would make a boy like you fall for a girl like me? What is it that binds us? And I think I know.

POSEY: You do?

RUTHIE: We'll both do anything to be happy.

(Pause)

POSEY: I love you.

RUTHIE: Will you do it?

POSEY: I love you. Say it back. Please. I need to hear it. Ruthie?

RUTHIE: You said he only kinda got away with it.

POSEY: Huh?

RUTHIE: The guy in the book, who murdered his landlady. You said he only kinda got away with it. Why just "kinda"?

POSEY: Because he couldn't live with hisself.

(Pause. RUTHIE looks at POSEY, both contemplating the act.)

(Suddenly, KEEGAN reappears, leaping from the stairs, in an instant gripping POSEY by his arms.)

KEEGAN: Gotcha now, bright boy!

POSEY: Help!

(KEEGAN puts POSEY in a severe full nelson. POSEY screams.)

KEEGAN: How's the bacon now, fruit?

RUTHIE: Keegan, you're breakin' his back!

KEEGAN: If you ever use that word again, by God—

POSEY: Mama!

KEEGAN: You hear me!

POSEY: Please mama!

RUTHIE: Keegan!

KEEGAN: When you gunna learn, bright boy!

POSEY: I'm sorry, brother! Don't break me, I'm beggin' ya! Don't break me, brother!

KEEGAN: You…will…respect…me!

(KEEGAN *intensifies the hold a moment longer, then lets go.* POSEY *collapses into a heap.*)

KEEGAN: Let's go.

RUTHIE: He's hurt.

KEEGAN: He's fine. Come on.

(KEEGAN *grabs* RUTHIE *by the hand and they rush out the front door, leaving it ajar as they go.* POSEY *weeps quietly on the floor. The dogs are barking again.* MARY MERLE *comes downstairs, wearing her nicest dress and holding a pair of scissors.*)

MARY MERLE: Heavens, all this racket. Can't get an ounce of quiet in this house. (*Sees* POSEY *on the floor.*) What're you doing down there, Posey? Another of your nightmare escapes? Keegan's right, bright boy: you're always hoot an' hollerin'—worse than Big Dog and Patty Cake. For the Lord's sake, stop dickerin' down there and cut this tag off my new dress. It's makin' me itch.

(*Just inside the front door,* BRODY *stands. He's an older black man. He holds a single suitcase and is dressed in a traveling suit.* MARY MERLE *sees him, startled stone solid. Pause.*)

MARY MERLE: Posey, on your feet, quick.

BRODY: The boy okay?

MARY MERLE: Posey, there's a—at the door. Why're you in my house?

BRODY: Name's Brody. I believe we spoke on the phone. This the Moon residence?

(*Blackout*)

Scene Two

(Thursday afternoon)

(Lights up on KEEGAN *and* RUTHIE *on the sofa making out.)*

RUTHIE: When I taste you…I lose control…like a drug…

KEEGAN: Uh-huh.

RUTHIE: It's like…sucking the flesh of…of a god…

KEEGAN: Yep. You gunna lose the shirt, babe?

RUTHIE: I told you, shirt stays on.

KEEGAN: Come on.

RUTHIE: Let's just smooch.

KEEGAN: Give us a bone, huh.

RUTHIE: Don't you gotta be at practice?

KEEGAN: Fifteen minutes. We got time.

RUTHIE: I said no.

KEEGAN: *(Breaking away, frustrated)* God dang, Ruthie, always sayin' that. I'm beginnin' to think you're a tease, Ruthie. When you gunna give an inch?

RUTHIE: You'll have your inch, Keegan Moon.

KEEGAN: One day, I better.

RUTHIE: That a threat?

KEEGAN: You know what Tommy Jinks said durin' 5th period?

RUTHIE: What'd Tommy Jinks say?

KEEGAN: He said after this mornin's paper I could probly stick it in any Dixie Cup in Balls.

RUTHIE: Tommy Jinks said that?

KEEGAN: He did.

RUTHIE: Well bless his little perv heart.

KEEGAN: Not every boy's got Bear Bryant barkin' after him.

RUTHIE: Don't I know.

KEEGAN: I could have my choosin'.

RUTHIE: Then why am I here, and not some other?

KEEGAN: Keep thinkin' you'll come around.

RUTHIE: Sometimes a girl's only hope hangs on how she chooses to come around.

KEEGAN: Hope at what?

RUTHIE: Somethin' more.

KEEGAN: Like what I got comin' to me?

RUTHIE: You might say.

KEEGAN: Mama says I was fated.

RUTHIE: She can't see straight, she fawns over you so.

KEEGAN: She's just thankful one of her boys turned out.

RUTHIE: Meaning you?

KEEGAN: Well, yeah. My brother's real queer. You'd see if you knew'im.

RUTHIE: When're you meetin' the Bear anyway?

KEEGAN: Coach Tutt says after the game.

RUTHIE: Where?

KEEGAN: Coach Tutt's office, then he's gunna visit the house.

RUTHIE: He's coming here?

KEEGAN: They say he only visits your house if he's real keen on you.

RUTHIE: Who else'll be here?

KEEGAN: Coach Tutt, I s'pose, and mama too.

RUTHIE: What about me?

KEEGAN: What's Bear Bryant want with you?

RUTHIE: I'm your girl.

KEEGAN: He's a football coach, Ruthie. He don't give a flip about courtship.

RUTHIE: They got cheerleadin' scholarships too, don't they? At the university?

KEEGAN: You thought all this out, ain'tcha?

RUTHIE: It's like this: you take me to this meetin' all sparklin' in my cheerleadin' attire—you know how I sparkle in my cheerleadin' attire. I sit beside you, perky and proud, while the Bear makes you a scholarship offer. And then you say, you say, "Gee-whiz, Coach Bryant, I'd love to accept, but when word gets out Bama offered me, all these other schools gunna offer too: Georgia, Auburn, Tennessee. And, well, I'd be a fool not to at least listen to such fine institutions as those." Then, the Bear, being shrewd like he is, he'll ask how he can sweetin' the pot.

KEEGAN: That's where you come in?

RUTHIE: We go to Tuscaloosa together. A package deal.

KEEGAN: You're off your head.

RUTHIE: I ain't either!

KEEGAN: You're askin' me to haggle Bear Bryant.

RUTHIE: I'm askin' you to commit to me, Keegan Moon. Will you do that?

KEEGAN: I can't grub the Bear!

RUTHIE: Then what's to become of me, huh? You go off to university, hot-shot punter. That can't happen, Keegan. I'm one of the last!

KEEGAN: Again with the hair—

RUTHIE: It's what sets me apart. Raquel Welch gets a thousand bucks—

KEEGAN: You told me 'bout Raquel Welch.

RUTHIE: A thousand bucks each time her hair gets photographed! Now what woulda become of Raquel Welch if she'd been stuck in Balls? My hair's got to be seen! Nobody in this town's ever gunna appreciate it like it deserves.

KEEGAN: Maybe we can come to an arrangement.

RUTHIE: Of what sort?

KEEGAN: I don't know. Maybe if—if you were to come around…

RUTHIE: Keegan Moon, you barefaced horn dog. So if I put out, you'll let me be at your meeting with the Bear.

KEEGAN: It's possible. What say?

RUTHIE: I'm not ready for that, Keegan.

KEEGAN: Other girls—

RUTHIE: I know what other girls do.

KEEGAN: Don't see what the problem is. You already got the reputation. Most of Balls thinks you're just the opposite of what you let on with me.

RUTHIE: Most of Balls can stick it.

KEEGAN: You don't have to go the whole hog with this. There's other ways, if you catch my meaning.

RUTHIE: Other ways?

KEEGAN: Other ways of gratifyin'.

RUTHIE: You mean—

KEEGAN: You know what I mean.

RUTHIE: The only other way I know of—

KEEGAN: Uh-huh.

RUTHIE: Jeez-Louise.

KEEGAN: It's a bargain, if you ask me.

RUTHIE: You little man-whore.

KEEGAN: You want to meet the Bear or not?

RUTHIE: Just this once, you hear me?

(KEEGAN *begins to unbutton and unzip his jeans.*)

RUTHIE: This ain't gunna be a regular thing. And I'm only gunna use my hand.

KEEGAN: Fine by me.

RUTHIE: Seems as though you always get what you want, Keegan Moon.

KEEGAN: Maybe I'm fated, like mama says.

RUTHIE: Or maybe you're just mean.

(KEEGAN *pulls off his jeans, leaving him in his undies.* RUTHIE *moves to reach inside, but* KEEGAN *stops her.*)

KEEGAN: Before you get to it, there's somethin' I gotta—I gotta say…

RUTHIE: What is it?

KEEGAN: Down there. What you're 'bout to find—it's incredible.

RUTHIE: Well, ain't you the bee's knees.

KEEGAN: I'm being for real, Ruthie.

RUTHIE: What? You hairless or somethin'?

KEEGAN: I got hair.

RUTHIE: You circumcised?

KEEGAN: 'Course I am. But, see, thing is—

RUTHIE: No. Don't say. I like mysteries. Lemme figure it out.

KEEGAN: Some mysteries you don't wanna solve on your own.

RUTHIE: My God, Keegan, it ain't like I ain't seen one before.

KEEGAN: Ruthie, I got three—

RUTHIE: Three?

KEEGAN: Testicles.

RUTHIE: Huh?

KEEGAN: Nuts. I got three of'em.

RUTHIE: Just when you think you know somebody.

KEEGAN: I thought I should alert you to it.

RUTHIE: You're a fine gentleman.

KEEGAN: They're the same as other nuts, just more of'em.

RUTHIE: Is that so?

KEEGAN: Yep. Mm. Well, you can get on with it.

RUTHIE: Get on with it?

KEEGAN: Proceed. Now that you know.

RUTHIE: I'm afraid.

KEEGAN: It's not so bad as you think. Here, lemme show you.

RUTHIE: Wait.

KEEGAN: Just take a peek.

RUTHIE: I ain't ready. I gotta prepare myself.

KEEGAN: It ain't a solar eclipse, Ruthie. Come on and look.

(KEEGAN *extends the elastic band on his undies, allowing* RUTHIE *to slowly, timidly, gaze downward into his nether region.*)

RUTHIE: Gracious alive...

KEEGAN: Welcome to my world.

RUTHIE: It's a minor miracle.

KEEGAN: Nothin' minor about it.

RUTHIE: One...two...three—

KEEGAN: They're all there.

RUTHIE: Four.

KEEGAN: What!

RUTHIE: Just kiddin'.

KEEGAN: Ain't funny, ain't at all.

(BRODY *begins to quietly make his way down the stairs. Sure not to be seen, he observes the couple from a distance.* RUTHIE *remains staring down* KEEGAN's *undies, astonished.*)

RUTHIE: How's somethin' like this happen?

KEEGAN: Lord knows. I's born this way.

RUTHIE: So you didn't grow it?

KEEGAN: Came out the womb with it.

RUTHIE: Your daddy have three nuts?

KEEGAN: Nope. Two.

RUTHIE: Your mama?

KEEGAN: Oh, you're gunna pay for that!

(KEEGAN *tackles* RUTHIE *to the floor. Playfully, they wrestle around and* KEEGAN *begins to tickle her.*)

KEEGAN: Tickle monster! Mooo-hahaha!

(BRODY *moves closer until he is standing only a few feet from them. Only* RUTHIE *sees him. She is flushed with panic but is so hysterical from the tickling, she can't get out a warning.*)

RUTHIE: K-K-K…Keeg…Keeg…a…there's a, a—

BRODY: *(Always a sunny, calm disposition)* Afternoon.

(At BRODY'S *voice,* KEEGAN *and* RUTHIE *rocket to their feet, whooping with alarm.* KEEGAN *struggles to get his jeans on.)*

KEEGAN: God dang! When he'd get here!

RUTHIE: He's standin' there all this time! I's tryin' to tell you!

KEEGAN: What're you doin' in our house!

BRODY: Name's Brody.

KEEGAN: *(Grabs the scissors from earlier)* I'll cut ya! I ain't afraid!

BRODY: And you are?

KEEGAN: I'm callin' the law! How'd you get in here?

BRODY: I was invited.

KEEGAN: Buncha bullcrap! Don't come near me!

BRODY: Lovely weather we're having.

KEEGAN: You'll give back whatever you took, understand!

BRODY: There's a bite of frost in the air.

KEEGAN: What're you after? Mama's jewelry?

BRODY: I live here now.

KEEGAN: What a fruit loop. You listenin' to this, Ruthie? Man thinks he lives here. It ain't a Holiday Inn, bucko.

BRODY: I'm the new boarder.

KEEGAN: The what?

BRODY: The new boarder. Answered your mother's ad. Paid the month's rent, cash down, this morning. She didn't tell you? See, there's no cause for alarm. You must be one of the sons. Name's Brody. *(Extends his hand)*

RUTHIE: Well, I'll be... *(She belts out in laughter.)*

KEEGAN: What...what the hell would you be rentin'?

BRODY: Spare room upstairs.

KEEGAN: Spare room? That's a closet.

BRODY: It's space enough.

KEEGAN: You knew 'bout this, Ruthie?

RUTHIE: *(Hooting still)* Sorta, kinda. Ain't it a riot? I wish I coulda seen Mother Moon's face when she laid eyes on you!

BRODY: Was very pale.

KEEGAN: How could mama do this to me?

RUTHIE: Where you from, mister?

BRODY: New York. Just passin' through a few days.

KEEGAN: Keeps getting' better! Biggest game of my life and I got a colored yankee livin' in my hallway closet!

RUTHIE: New York City?

BRODY: Yes mam.

RUTHIE: Ain't that somethin'.

KEEGAN: What's mama thinkin'?

RUTHIE: She said it was to get your daddy's guns cleaned.

KEEGAN: She must have loved him somethin' fierce.

RUTHIE: Don't you got practice?

KEEGAN: I reckon it'll do me good to punt something! I'm so mad!

BRODY: You're a real ball of fury, aren't you?

KEEGAN: *(Raging)* What's that supposed to mean!

BRODY:Okay then.

KEEGAN: I don't wantcha in my room. Ever. You understand?

BRODY: Ground rules have been explained.

KEEGAN: I mean it, keep outta my way.

BRODY: You won't know I'm here.

KEEGAN: We gotta split, Ruthie.

RUTHIE: I'll stay.

KEEGAN: But you always watch me practice.

RUTHIE: I never met someone from New York.

KEEGAN: This ain't like you.

RUTHIE: I'll be waitin' for you after practice. We'll go see that two-headed cow down at the fair tonight.

KEEGAN: You promise?

RUTHIE: I do, I promise.

KEEGAN: *(Kisses* RUTHIE, *then a last word to* BRODY *as he heads out.)* Stay outta my room.

BRODY: Stay outta my closet.

*(*KEEGAN *exits. Long pause.* RUTHIE *flashes* BRODY *a big smile.)*

RUTHIE: Ever since he got word of that cow he won't let it rest. Been at me every night this week to see the dang thing. I imagine ya'll ain't got no use for two-headed cows in New York, New York. I heard ya'll never even gotta eat at the same restaurant more than once, on account there's all them choices. We only got the one McDonald's.

BRODY: I noticed.

RUTHIE: What business you got in Balls, mister?

BRODY: I'm a scientist.

RUTHIE: What sort?

BRODY: A pedologist.

RUTHIE: Podiatrist?

BRODY: Pedologist.

RUTHIE: Which is—?

BRODY: I study soil.

RUTHIE: What you want with Balls, Alabama?

BRODY: I'm interested in your red dirt.

RUTHIE: We got plenty of that.

BRODY: The highest concentration anywhere. Right here.

RUTHIE: We're the dirtiest.

BRODY: I'm collecting samples.

RUTHIE: A few bags full?

BRODY: More. Much more. Enough to last. It's not easy getting here.

RUTHIE: It's not easy leaving either.

BRODY: Name's Brody.

RUTHIE: Mr Brody, I'm Ruthie. *(Pause)* I ain't ever been alone with your kind before.

BRODY: And what kind would that be?

RUTHIE: Take your pick.

(POSEY enters through the front door, sees RUTHIE and BRODY.)

POSEY: Hey.

RUTHIE: Posey! I been waitin' for you, Posey.

POSEY: What're you two doin'?

BRODY: You met Mr Brody?

POSEY: *(Gruffly)* I met'im.

RUTHIE: He's from New York City.

POSEY: So he says.

BRODY: Last I saw of you, you were in a bad way.

POSEY: I'm fine now.

BRODY: Young man could hardly walk.

RUTHIE: He's from New York, Posey. New York, New York.

BRODY: City so nice—

RUTHIE: They named twice.

BRODY: Right on, little lady.

POSEY: Alright, just cut it out. I may be from Balls, buddy, but I wasn't born yesterday. I know who you are. I've seen the lights, I've heard the engines.

BRODY: You lost me.

POSEY: Late at night. In the sky above.

BRODY: Sky above?

POSEY: You know what I'm sayin'.

BRODY: I truly do not.

POSEY: If you're really from New York, what's a taxi cost these days?

RUTHIE: What tree you sniffin' up, Posey?

POSEY: Ruthie, this ain't a man standin' before us. He's an alien from outer space. His spaceship's been visitin' this house for months.

RUTHIE: Posey, please.

POSEY: Now he's taken a human form to get behind these doors.

BRODY: This is a theory of yours?

POSEY: It all adds up. Appears outta thin air and don't even know the rate of cab fare. And he's from New York? Right!

RUTHIE: Ask him somethin' else.

POSEY: He ain't gunna know.

RUTHIE: Just ask him.

POSEY: Alright then. What's the colors of the New York City flag?

BRODY: I didn't know the city had a flag.

POSEY: See! Alien!

BRODY: Where'd you get this stuff?

POSEY: Checked a book outta the library today. *(Pulls book from his bag.) A Southerner's Guide to Gotham.*

RUTHIE: Ask'im somethin' easy.

POSEY: I'm tellin' you, ain't no use. He's a phony.

BRODY: Orange, white and blue. Colors of the city flag. Orange, white and blue. Like the Mets. Satisfied?

POSEY: Well, well. You was briefed by your alien cronies.

BRODY: Just came to me.

POSEY: Uh-huh, real likely. Then tell me the boundaries of Central Park.

BRODY: 59th Street on the south, 110th on the north.

POSEY: What's the front of the public library known for?

BRODY: It sits between the lions.

POSEY: I see you was briefed real good. Crafty. It's clear your alien brain's been programmed in anticipation of such a grillin'.

RUTHIE: Seems human to me.

BRODY: Posey, you're nearly as pleasant as your brother. *(Moving to exit)* Well, so listen, this has been fun and all, but I got supplies to pick up.

POSEY: What sort of supplies?

RUTHIE: Mr Brody's a scientist.

POSEY: Yeah, I bet.

RUTHIE: A proctologist.

BRODY: Pedologist.

RUTHIE: Right. He's come to study our red dirt.

POSEY: Probably he's wanting to harvest it, take it back to his home planet. I bet it has some kind of mineral in it his alien civilization needs to survive.

(BRODY has stopped in his tracks. Very still. Pause. He turns to POSEY, his countenance changed, more intense, severe. The lights flicker a moment.)

BRODY: How'd you know that?

POSEY: Know what?

BRODY: About the dirt.

POSEY: Just a guess.

BRODY: A guess?

POSEY: Yeah.

BRODY: A guess.

RUTHIE: Posey, what've you done?

POSEY: A *wild* guess.

BRODY: It's correct.

RUTHIE: Holy shit.

BRODY: Unfortunately.

RUTHIE: Oh god.

POSEY: Quiet, Ruthie.

BRODY: The red dirt—it's our energy source. It fuels our planet.

POSEY: Take all you want.

BRODY: We visit every few hundred years to collect it. If it was ever jeopardized—

RUTHIE: We won't tell!

POSEY: She's right, we won't! Who'd believe us?

BRODY: I can't risk it. You have to die now.

RUTHIE: What!

POSEY: Now hang on.

BRODY: You left me no choice.

RUTHIE: Please, please mister—

POSEY: How you gunna do it?

BRODY: Vaporization.

POSEY: *(Can't help but be a bit intrigued)* Really? You can do that?

BRODY: All that'll be left of you both is a drop of water.

POSEY: That's pretty far out.

RUTHIE: Posey! You're not helping!

POSEY: Well it is!

RUTHIE: Wait wait, we have a secret too.

POSEY: Yeah, we do! We do?

RUTHIE: I'll tell you ours, and you can use it as leverage against us telling yours!

BRODY: You mean about sticking your hand down that punter's pants?

RUTHIE: No, a better one.

POSEY: You stuck your hand down Keegan's pants?

RUTHIE: Not now, Posey!

POSEY: How could you?

RUTHIE: Posey!

BRODY: She was ready and willing.

RUTHIE: Mind your own, spaceman!

POSEY: I'm devastated.

RUTHIE: It meant nothing.

BRODY: What about this secret?

RUTHIE: Listen, tomorrow night, we're going to assassinate Bear Bryant.

BRODY: Okay. So?

POSEY: Did you hear what she said?

BRODY: Who in the hell is Bear Bryant?

POSEY: He's a football coach.

RUTHIE: He's a god in these parts.

BRODY: Your god is a football coach?

POSEY: Point is, you couldn't think up a better cover.

RUTHIE: All the focus will be on Keegan, and the game, and the Bear's visit.

POSEY: No one'll care, or notice, what's happening to our red dirt.

RUTHIE: It's the perfect smoke screen.

POSEY: Why ruin it by making a couple of no-name kids disappear?

(Pause. BRODY *bursts into laughter.)*

BRODY: I'm just messing with you!

RUTHIE: Huh?

BRODY: I'm no alien! I'm from Bushwick!

POSEY: You was winding us up?

BRODY: Sure I was. There's no such thing as aliens.

POSEY: How do you know?

BRODY: First of all, if I was an alien in disguise, why the hell would I come to Alabama as a black man?

RUTHIE: He makes a point.

BRODY: You two really going to murder that coach?

RUTHIE: Assassinate.

POSEY: Of course not. Just talk.

BRODY: Probably better be. Things are never so desperate to dictate something like that. Anyway, I'd better get those supplies. Start my digging. I wouldn't want to keep the mothership waiting. *(He resumes his laughter as he exits out the front door.)*

POSEY: So?

RUTHIE: So?

POSEY: Is it true?

RUTHIE: Posey—

POSEY: You were willing to be with Keegan like that.

RUTHIE: It wouldn't have meant nothin'.

POSEY: It would've to me.

RUTHIE: For us to follow through on the plan, we need to be in the room. I had to be sure.

POSEY: I can't stand the thought.

RUTHIE: Nothing happened.

POSEY: Promise you won't be with him like that.

RUTHIE: Okay.

POSEY: Say it.

RUTHIE: I promise.

POSEY: I don't want—

RUTHIE: I said I promise. *(She kisses him gently.)* Sit down.

POSEY: Why?

RUTHIE: Just sit down.

(Unsure, POSEY sits where KEEGAN sat earlier. RUTHIE unbuttons and unzips his jeans.)

POSEY: What's happenin'?

RUTHIE: I'm about to do somethin' for you I ain't done to no one. Not even your brother.

POSEY: But—

RUTHIE: Shhh. Sit back now. Relax. Worry about nothin'. I'll make you a memory.

(RUTHIE starts to reach inside POSEY's pants.)

POSEY: Wait. Before you do, I should—there's somethin' you should know.

RUTHIE: Know about what?

POSEY: What you're about to find. Down there.

RUTHIE: You gotta be kiddin'.

(Blackout)

END OF ACT ONE

ACT TWO

(At rise:)

(MOON family home. Empty, dark late. Quiet. As before, the rumbling comes and the beams of light shine in, this time revealing the figure of BRODY, in half shadow, on the sofa. He stares ahead, stern and steely, with a pickaxe sitting over his lap. After reaching their climax, the sounds and beams fade to stillness. Lights to complete black.)

Scene One

(Friday morning)

(Laughter. Lights up. BRODY and MARY MERLE over breakfast at the kitchen table. MARY MERLE wears a fine dress. The pickaxe is propped up in the corner of the living room. The mood is jovial. MARY MERLE is telling jokes.)

MARY MERLE: Here's another one, a good clean one. A mama goes to the door of her son's room and says, "Time for church!" The son says "I'm not going!" The mama says, "Why not?" Son says, "I'll give you two reasons: first, they don't like me, and, second, I don't like them!" The mama says, "I'll give you two reasons why YOU ARE going: first, you're forty-nine years old and, second, you're the pastor!"

(BRODY and MARY MERLE laugh.)

BRODY: He's the pastor!

MARY MERLE: Ain't that the kicker!

BRODY: It is, it is!

MARY MERLE: Had me rollin' on the floor when Deacon Billy first told it.

BRODY: Too much..

MARY MERLE: Ain't it.

BRODY: Oh me. *(Pushing his plate away, finished)* Mrs. Moon, I'm not sure what I just ate, but it was delicious.

MARY MERLE: Cheese grits. Must be exotic to a yankee like you.

BRODY: You don't know the half of it.

(BRODY and MARY MERLE laugh. POSEY comes down the stairs. Grabs his book bag, ostensibly preparing for school, but primarily observing the interaction between his mother and BRODY.)

MARY MERLE: You're a good egg, Mr Brody. Not what I expected when we spoke by phone, but you're a good egg.

BRODY: Pleased to hear.

MARY MERLE: I'm sorry how we got off on the wrong foot yesterday. Didn't mean nothin' by it. Y'know, I got lots of black friends.

BRODY: Me too.

MARY MERLE: I reckon relations is different where you're from.

BRODY: Some ways, yes. Other ways, no.

MARY MERLE: Flip on the news and there's always whites and coloreds somewhere in the South raisin' Cain. Dunno why feelings run so raw in these parts. Posey says the South is the American id.

BRODY: What's an id?

MARY MERLE: How's Posey say it?... *(Recalling his exact words)* Where our most urgent truths simmer and fester, unrestricted.

BRODY: That's educated talk.

MARY MERLE: It's Shakespeare.

POSEY: Freud.

MARY MERLE: More coffee, Mr Brody?

BRODY: I've had plenty, thank you.

MARY MERLE: *(Drolly)* Posey, you seen any of them Martians last night?

POSEY: No, ma'am. Martians? Uh-uh. Nope.

MARY MERLE: He thinks he sees Martians.

BRODY: You don't say.

MARY MERLE: The thought that aliens would come to Balls, that we're being watched. I've had it up to here with his ooga-booga. Some mornings he won't shut up about it.

BRODY: He seems pretty tight-lipped about it this morning.

MARY MERLE: Probly on account of you being here.

BRODY: Maybe that has something to do with it.

MARY MERLE: You being bashful, Posey? Go on, tell us about your little green men.

(POSEY rushes up the stairs.)

MARY MERLE: Such an odd boy.

BRODY: Just young is all.

MARY MERLE: Well, don't let me keep you. I know you got a long day of science ahead. Please, take all the red dirt you want. That your pickaxe over yonder?

BRODY: Why, yes mam, forgive me. Meant to put it in my room last night.

MARY MERLE: No harm. You gunna use it to dig?

BRODY: That's the plan.

MARY MERLE: It's a big day, you know. Met my celebrated son yet?

BRODY: The boy who kicks.

MARY MERLE: Bear Bryant's comin' down to extend him a scholarship.

BRODY: I heard. That's wonderful.

MARY MERLE: Me and Keegan's got us an interview with the *Balls Gazette* after breakfast. They're doin' a feature on the family for the Sunday edition.

BRODY: Dressed up for it, I see.

MARY MERLE: They say they may be wantin' a family photo. Naturally, I asked Posey to come too but he says—

POSEY: *(Calling from upstairs)* I'd rather have my toes chopped off and fed to me raw!

MARY MERLE: So the family'll be incomplete. 'Course, in the grand picture, the family's been incomplete nearly three years now. Perhaps you heard what became of Mr Moon.

BRODY: No mam, I haven't

MARY MERLE: Fell into the feed grinder.

BRODY: I'm terribly sorry.

MARY MERLE: He's up at God now. These are his guns on the wall, y'know.

BRODY: I assumed.

MARY MERLE: One of the finest collections in the region. But you know what really sets them apart.

BRODY: What's that?

MARY MERLE: Ain't a one of'em been fired.

BRODY: That the truth?

MARY MERLE: Properly loaded but never fired. Forney had'em since we met.

BRODY: In high school, I imagine?

MARY MERLE: Balls High, Class of '55.

BRODY: Figured so. You look mighty young to be a widower.

MARY MERLE: Why, Mr Brody, you're a Mississippi sweet-talker.

BRODY: I don't mean to pry.

MARY MERLE: Not a bit. Been ages since someone asked. In the start, I was best friends with his high school sweetheart, see. Donna Fay Coogan was her name. Gettin' close to Forney was the only reason I got on with her. She didn't know how good she had it, but I did. Useta we'd meet behind the Winn Dixie— his friends, her friends—to hang around. All the boys'd smoke their cigarettes but Forney, being a star athlete, never smoked. Uh-uh. He favored bananas. So I'd carry a spare banana in my purse and when the others'd light up I'd offer it to Forney. He'd take it and say, "Why, Mary Merle, perhaps it's you I should be walkin' home tonight." Every time, never failed, "Why, Mary Merle, perhaps it's you I should be walkin' home tonight." Such a boy. Then come our senior year and Donna Fay Coogan came down with the lupus and died. I wudn't happy about it, but I wudn't sad neither. Way I see it, this ain't the world God wanted, and you gotta make do with the breaks you get, however they come. Funeral was that spring. After the service, I find my way to Forney and pull a banana from my purse. And he says, "Why, Mary Merle, perhaps it's

you…." And he stops cold, like he's hit by a meteor or
somethin'. That's all he says. All he hadta say. I had'im.
It took a tragedy, but I had'im. We was married later
that year and I was officially vested Mrs. Forney James
Moon the Junior. He took work at the packaging plant.
Twins was born. And, for 16 years, our life was lived.
Till the Orange Bowl. It'n that somethin'? A little ole
football game took'im from me. He drinks himself
silly, stumbles out to the old barn. The next morning
I hear Posey screamin'. I run out, take him in my
arms, and see what's left of my husband. He looked
a jigsaw of hisself—like wet plaster and meat sauce.
But, no doubting, it was him: Mr Forney James Moon
the Junior. The polite boy who ate my bananas. It was
that moment, I think, seeing his remains, with Posey
wailing in my arms, it was that moment I became old.
And I'd never even learned how to drive.

KEEGAN: *(From off, upstairs)* God dang it all! Mama, I
cain't tie my necktie!

MARY MERLE: Oh, he's up already. I's plannin' to serve
him cheese grits in bed.

BRODY: First-class.

MARY MERLE: He deserves it. His day.

KEEGAN: *(From off, upstairs)* Don't we still got some of
daddy's clip-ons!

POSEY: *(Coming down the stairs)* Good thing he can punt.
He's plumb dumb in everything else.

MARY MERLE: I can't tie them things, and I done gave
all them clip-ons to the Goodwill. Posey, go help your
brother tie his tie.

POSEY: I really shouldn't.

MARY MERLE: Why on earth not?

POSEY: 'Cause I'd choke him.

MARY MERLE: Well try not to!

KEEGAN: *(From off, upstairs)* Mama, help! The knot won't keep!

MARY MERLE: Be right there, baby boy! He's so grumpy when he ain't woke up yet. Posey, please. I want him lookin' nice for the photo. You're the only one knows how.

POSEY: Let'im keep at it. Maybe he'll discover his opposable thumb.

BRODY: I could help.

MARY MERLE: Help how?

BRODY: I can tie a tie.

MARY MERLE: You?

BRODY: Be happy to tie it for him.

POSEY: That'll wake him up.

MARY MERLE: I'd sure appreciate it, Mr Brody. This photo commands formality. It might be historical one day.

BRODY: Had a sorta rocky start with the boy. Maybe this'll help patch things.

MARY MERLE: Just go on up to his room.

POSEY: You sure that's a good idea, mama?

MARY MERLE: Keegan'll be so thankful.

BRODY: Just let me grab my pickaxe—put that away while I'm up there. Many thanks for the cheese grits, Mrs Moon.

MARY MERLE: Weren't nothin' at all.

KEEGAN: *(From off, upstairs)* Mama!

MARY MERLE: Comin'!

(MARY MERLE *nods to* BRODY. *He winks and heads up. To*
POSEY.)

MARY MERLE: You tended them dogs?

POSEY: I fed'em the last two mornings. It's Keegan's
turn.

MARY MERLE: Keeg's got things to concentrate on!

POSEY: Like his tie?

MARY MERLE: Like the family legacy. Go feed'em their
breakfast!

POSEY: This really beats all, you know that. Shame on
you and all of Balls for toppin' your pedestals with
false kings.

MARY MERLE: False kings? Keegan's been by your side
since conception.

POSEY: Suffocatin' me senseless.

MARY MERLE: Two sperms travelin' through my
insides and, against all odds, both findin' you an egg.
The likelihood. You'd think that'd be grounds for some
kind of bond. Instead, all you got is spite and envy.

POSEY: I don't wanna fight. Really I don't.

MARY MERLE: You even gunna be at the game tonight?

POSEY: No mam, I'm not.

MARY MERLE: Honor the rock from which you're hewn,
bright boy.

POSEY: I said I don't wanna argue no more.

MARY MERLE: Do you know what tonight could mean
for this family?

POSEY: False glory.

MARY MERLE: Posey, you better be at this game.

(POSEY *moves to exit through the sliding door.*)

MARY MERLE: Where you goin'? Don't walk away from me.

POSEY: Thought you wanted me to feed the dogs.

MARY MERLE: I want you at the game! You hear me?

(POSEY *walks out.*)

MARY MERLE: Posey! Bright boy!

(MARY MERLE *takes a few steps as if to follow after him. Halts. Goes to the kitchen, pulls out her bottle of Old Crow and a glass, slams a shot. Exhales a deep breath, savoring. Returns bottle and glass.* KEEGAN *barrels down the stairs.*)

KEEGAN: Mama! Mama! Call the sheriff!

MARY MERLE: Why? What's got into you?

KEEGAN: He tried to kill me!

MARY MERLE: Who did?

KEEGAN: The Negro yankee! He tried to kill me!

MARY MERLE: Calm down. What're you sayin'?

KEEGAN: I's in my room, tying my tie in the mirror, and I seen'im comin' at me from behind with a pickaxe!

MARY MERLE: He wasn't tryin' to kill you.

KEEGAN: Was too! I seen'im!

MARY MERLE: I sent'im up to help with your tie.

KEEGAN: With a pickaxe?

MARY MERLE: It's his diggin' tool.

KEEGAN: He's aimin' to take it to my skull!

MARY MERLE: Sit down and cool off. Lemme gitcha some juice.

KEEGAN: Never seen such a sight—a colored with a pickaxe, in my own room!

MARY MERLE: Mr Brody's a scientist.

KEEGAN: Daddy'd never approve of bringin' a stranger in this house, even if it was to clean his guns.

MARY MERLE: Somebody's gotta tie that tie. Now you drink this and go up apologize.

KEEGAN: No way I'm gunna apologize. Anyways, I couldn't if I wanted.

MARY MERLE: How come?

KEEGAN: I popped him a good one.

MARY MERLE: You hit Mr Brody?

KEEGAN: I's defendin' myself!

MARY MERLE: Gracious!

KEEGAN: Laid him out. Think I broke his nose.

MARY MERLE: Who's gunna tie your tie now?

KEEGAN: Someone walks into my room with a pickaxe and I'm gunna sock the sucker!

MARY MERLE: Oh Keegan, this is bad. Bad! *(Exiting up the stairs)* Mr Brody? You alright? You need some ice? Mr Brody?

(KEEGAN chugs his juice. Decides to give his tie another try, mumbling directions as he attempts to tie the knot.)

KEEGAN: Twice over...once under...tighten and straighten. *(A botched result)* Friggin' hell!

(POSEY enters from the sliding door.)

KEEGAN: Oh. Mornin', fruit. Tell me, what's it like to have a brother who's cock of the walk?

POSEY: You got the cock part right.

KEEGAN: You better start being nice to me.

POSEY: Wasn't Brody gunna fix your tie?

KEEGAN: Apparently.

POSEY: What happened?

KEEGAN: I clubbed him one.

POSEY: You didn't.

KEEGAN: Out cold.

POSEY: There was blood?

KEEGAN: Lots of it. It was spillin' all over.

POSEY: You shouldn't have done that.

KEEGAN: He had a pickaxe. He was in my room.

POSEY: Who'll tie your tie now?

KEEGAN: May have to go without. Mama's 'bout to drive me batty about this photo, makin' me get all hussied up. What's the sense in it? I punt footballs.

POSEY: Ruthie coming over? She's usually here by now.

KEEGAN: *(Attempting to tie again)* Likely not. She's sore at me, I think.

POSEY: What for?

KEEGAN: None your business.

POSEY: When'd you last see her?

KEEGAN: We went to see that two-headed cow last night. Things got rowdy.

POSEY: She okay?

KEEGAN: She's fine.

POSEY: Did you hurt her?

KEEGAN: I said she's fine.

POSEY: What'd you do?

KEEGAN: Can't much blame me, all the teasing she does.

POSEY: What'd you do?

KEEGAN: *(Botched the tie again)* Dang it! These things are impossible!

(Pause)

POSEY: *(Seething, but managing to conceal it)* I'll tie it for you.

KEEGAN: You pullin' my leg?

POSEY: I'd like to tie it.

KEEGAN: You'd do that for me?

POSEY: You're right. All you got coming to you, I oughta be nicer.

KEEGAN: I sure appreciate it.

POSEY: No bother. Go ahead and slip it around your neck.

(KEEGAN *and* POSEY *stand facing each other. Throughout the next sequence,* POSEY *straightens* KEEGAN's *collar and fastens his top button before beginning to slowly tie his tie.)*

KEEGAN: Awful kind of you, bright boy.

POSEY: I'd prefer we do this in silence.

KEEGAN: Real sorry I nearly broke your back yesterday.

POSEY: Just shut up, really.

KEEGAN: Man oh man, you shoulda seen this cow last night at the fair. This thing, it had two heads alright. But it was all distorted, y'know. Unclean. Eyes where the mouth goes. Mouths where the ears go. Like the two heads was growin' outta each other. Just disgustin'. Droolin' and wheezin', pus oozing out its scabs, flies all around. Just wallowin' there. Well, I wasn't havin' it. Felt jipped. Me and Ruthie paid two bucks for this? Hell naw. So I remembered I'd bought me these poppers—you know them firecrackers that pop when you throw'em on the ground. Well, I still had me several in my pocket. So I start throwin' them next to the cow's cage. Pop! Pop! That sure woke the fat heffer up. Sombitch starts havin' this fit, y'know.

Its eyes go goggly and its tongue starts lashin' at the
air. Shittin' and pissin' itself, no clue what's goin' on.
Pop! Pop! Crowd's laughin' and cheerin' me on, while
this cow starts shakin' like it's going into seizure! And
I keep tossin' them suckers, every last one of'em, till I
run clean out. Pop! Pop! Pop! And everybody applauds
and shakes my hand for the show they done witnessed.
If that cow's got an ounce of mind left, it ain't soon
gunna forget Keegan Moon!

(POSEY *tightens the knot into a choke and swipes* KEEGAN'S
feet from under him, taking him down hard. POSEY *then
wraps the tie around* KEEGAN'S *neck, securing his brother
in a strained choke hold.*)

POSEY: How 'bout now, baby boy?

KEEGAN: *(Gasping through the choke)* Mama, mama—

POSEY: This part of your destiny? Huh, jackass? This
fated too?

KEEGAN: Can't breathe—

POSEY: My chokin' the shit outta you the mornin' of
your big day?

KEEGAN: Mama—

POSEY: Admit you took it.

KEEGAN: Go to hell.

POSEY: *(Tightening his hold)* Admit you took it.

KEEGAN: Don't know what—

POSEY: Say it, or I swear to Christ, you'll never punt
again.

KEEGAN: Honestly, I don't know what—

POSEY: The womb.

KEEGAN: Womb—

POSEY: In the womb.

KEEGAN: You're killin' me—

POSEY: Say what you took!

KEEGAN: Posey—

POSEY: Say it!

KEEGAN: Nut—I took your nut, Posey!

POSEY: Why?

KEEGAN: Let go, you said you would—

POSEY: No I didn't. Tell me why.

KEEGAN: So I'd have three...so you'd have one—

POSEY: And the rest is destiny.

KEEGAN: Got too much blood in my head—

POSEY: I always knew why mama said we came out wrestlin'. 'Cause you had what I's owed. A thief, just like I been sayin'. Apologize!

KEEGAN: No—

POSEY: *(Tightens hold to breaking point)* Yes! Apologize, brother, for thieving me!

KEEGAN: I won't—

POSEY: Why not?

KEEGAN: 'CAUSE I AIN'T SORRY!

(KEEGAN unleashes a burst of energy, lifting himself up with a monstrous grunt, elbowing POSEY and then flipping him on his back. Frantic, KEEGAN begins to choke POSEY with his hands.)

KEEGAN: 'Cause I ain't sorry! I ain't! I ain't sorry! I ain't sorry! I ain't sorry! I ain't sorry! I ain't! I ain't...

(KEEGAN would kill POSEY in this moment but is overcome by a coughing fit and his own exhaustion. He lets go of POSEY's neck, slides off him to the floor. Both brothers lie mostly limp, wheezing. A lengthy pause.)

POSEY: *(Mustering the breath to speak)* All my life I watched you. You never knew, but I's there. I'd sneak around. Behind corners. Under bleachers. Blending into the horizon. Away from crowds. To see you. To see the boy-god kick the flesh of swine. Riveted, I was, like all the rest. At how you belong, how perfectly suited you are to time and place. *(Tenderly)* I hate you.

KEEGAN: I hate you too.

(Pause. MARY MERLE comes down the stairs.)

MARY MERLE: Well, he's locked hisself in his closet. Won't even answer me!

KEEGAN: Probly upset.

POSEY: Do ya think?

MARY MERLE: *(Despite the boys flailed on the floor, all she sees is the tie.)* Your tie! It's tied! Howdy do! Look atcha, baby boy. A Dapper Dan if I ever seen one!

KEEGAN: I feel stuffy.

MARY MERLE: You look a million bucks, you do. What're you two doin'? Wrasslin' again? Up, both of ya. We gotta get down there, Keegan. Newspaper wants to do it at the high school, with Coach Tutt.

KEEGAN: Fine.

MARY MERLE: Cheese grits'll keep till tomorrow. Get your bag. *(Goes to POSEY, smiling)* I'm glad you listened to me, bright boy. Tying your brother's tie on his big day. Real brotherly of you, Posey. Keegan, thank your brother.

KEEGAN: But mama!

MARY MERLE: Keegan, I asked you to thank your brother.

KEEGAN: He don't deserve no thanks!

MARY MERLE: He tied your tie! Otherwise, you'd look a damn monkey in this photo! Now thank'im!

KEEGAN: Okay! Jeez! *(Pause)* Thanks—fruit.

MARY MERLE: Good enough. Small steps. Posey, we're off! Maybe we'll see you at the game tonight? So happy you come around, bright boy! Any last words for your brother?

POSEY: Don't drop the ball.

MARY MERLE: Ain't that sweet. Let's go, sweetheart.

(KEEGAN *and* MARY MERLE *exit out the front door.* KEEGAN *glares back, slamming the door as he goes.* POSEY, *alone, sits on the sofa, processing what's happened. From upstairs, a crash is heard. Heavy, violent, intense pounding. It continues.* POSEY *rises and moves, cautiously, to the bottom of the stairs for a closer listen. After a moment, the clamor ceases. Pause. A tapping comes from the sliding door, startling* POSEY. *It's* RUTHIE, *dressed in her cheerleading uniform. She has a black eye and busted lip.)*

RUTHIE: They gone?

POSEY: Yeah. You okay?

RUTHIE: *(Wryly)* Never better.

POSEY: Did he—?

RUTHIE: Is it noticeable?

POSEY: Am I being honest?

RUTHIE: I got to be at the pep rally.

POSEY: What happened?

RUTHIE: What's it look like?

POSEY: He did this to you?

RUTHIE: Last night, after the fair. He decided he was gunna have me, no matter what. Felt like he could take whatever he wanted. He forced hisself on me. So

I grabbed his nuts, squeezed and twisted as hard as I could.

POSEY: All three of them?

RUTHIE: Yep, the whole caboodle. Had him yelping like a bitch. Had no choice. That's when he hit me.

(POSEY *and* RUTHIE *embrace.*)

RUTHIE: That two-headed cow—it's terrifying.

POSEY: I know.

RUTHIE: After Keegan let loose his poppers and the crowd swooped him away, I stayed behind.

POSEY: With the cow.

RUTHIE: Just me and him, alone. You ever heard an animal scream before?

POSEY: No.

RUTHIE: Screamin', idle in the night, no one there to hear it but me. There's so much despair bound up in cages. If it was ever set loose, it'd deafen the world.

POSEY: Tonight, when it's done, we'll take daddy's old pick-up. It still runs.

RUTHIE: And go where?

POSEY: Where you wanna go?

RUTHIE: Somewhere far.

POSEY: Fine then.

RUTHIE: I don't think I can hear that scream again.

POSEY: You won't. One way or another, you won't.

RUTHIE: We really gunna do this?

(POSEY *moves to the Colt .44 mounted on the wall. He pulls it down and places it in his bag. He and* RUTHIE *share a moment of solemn resolve, then exit out the front door.)*

(After a moment, BRODY comes down the stairs. Something is off about him. He seems dazed, mechanical almost, as if his wiring has been thrown off. He holds his suitcase, and pickaxe, and is dressed in his suit. There appears to be granulated blood encrusted on his nose and upper lip. As he comes down the stairs, he repeats phrases he's already spoken, seemingly at random.)

BRODY: Name's Brody... This the Moon residence?... Lovely weather we're having... There's a bite of frost in the air...I'm the new boarder... Paid the month's rent, cash down, this morning...I'm a scientist...I study soil... Enough to last... Like the Mets... It's our energy source... It fuels our planet...I'm no alien! I'm from Bushwick! ...Bushwick...Bushwick... *(He stares out with a wide-eyed, empty expression.)*

(Blackout)

Scene Two

(Friday night)

(Lights up. Lightning, thunder. Outside, a hard rain pours, dogs bark. The power is out. BRODY is sitting on the sofa, in shadows, stock-still, with his suitcase and pickaxe placed neatly beside him. The only sources of light are a lantern next to BRODY and slivers of moonlight that trickle into the home as the rain gradually wanes. BRODY wears the same expression as before. In the kitchen, the phone begins to ring. And ring. And ring. And ring some more. BRODY doesn't react to the ringing at all. Finally, MARY MERLE barrels through the front door, rushing in from the weather, sprightly and spirited, carrying a cake in a box. MARY MERLE doesn't notice BRODY.)

MARY MERLE: Gracious me, the clouds done burst wide open! *(Tries the light switch. Nothing)* Well, if that don't beat all... *(Answers phone in kitchen.)* Hello? Oh, evenin',

Mr Maze. No, they ain't here yet. They're still at the stadium. I came on home to get things set up. Why, I surely will pass along congratulations. Wasn't he though? I am. Proud enough to pop. Thank yooouuu. Evenin', Mr Maze.

(MARY MERLE *hangs up. Puts cake on kitchen table. Begins to take off raincoat. Barely gets it off before the phone rings again. As she speaks, she begins to pull out plates and forks.*)

MARY MERLE: This Mary Merle. Clarice, I thought you'd be callin'. I tell ya, a gully washer. Think all of Balls gone black. No, he ain't. Still at the stadium. Phone's ringin' off the hook. What's that? You don't say. The two-headed cow? It got loose? Got spooked by the thunder, huh. Well, I'll be. I'm sure it'll turn up. Alright, Clarice. Bye now.

(MARY MERLE *hangs up the phone. Almost immediately, it begins to ring again. She takes it off the hook. Begins to search for her candles. She sees* BRODY.)

MARY MERLE: Mr Brody? That you?

BRODY: (*Speaks steadily, but with little animation*) Yes mam.

MARY MERLE: You leavin' already?

BRODY: Yes mam.

MARY MERLE: You're paid up till the end of the month.

BRODY: Found an empty lot out by the county line. Plenty of samples there for me to collect and be on my way.

MARY MERLE: But on a night like this?

BRODY: It's no worry.

MARY MERLE: Well, you're the scientist. Let me refund you some of your rent.

BRODY: You keep it.

MARY MERLE: To tell you the truth, Mr Brody, I'll miss your company.

BRODY: Say, how'd that boy of yours do tonight?

MARY MERLE: Oh fine, real fine! You're kind for askin'! The game of his life!

BRODY: Game of his life, you say.

MARY MERLE: Had him six punts in all, each of'em went fifty yards or more. His last went for sixty-one. A spectacle to behold.

BRODY: And Bear Bryant was there?

MARY MERLE: Clad in his houndstooth. Oozing with presence.

BRODY: You met him?

MARY MERLE: Met'im? I touched him. With this hand here. It smells of legend.

BRODY: Lucky lady, you.

MARY MERLE: He offered Keegan like we was hoping. Offered him on the spot. Bear Bryant wants my boy, my own kin.

BRODY: He accept?

MARY MERLE: On the spot. My boy's gunna play for the Alabama Crimson Tide.

BRODY: Oh, what a future he has in store.

MARY MERLE: I'm sorry he socked you, Mr Brody.

BRODY: All's forgotten.

MARY MERLE: I'm glad you understand. I reckon this the happiest I been since before Forney passed. You wanna drink? A shot of Old Crow?

BRODY: Best not.

MARY MERLE: It's a celebration. You're drinkin'. I insist. *(Crosses to kitchen, pouring two shots)* Bought Keegan his favorite chocolate cake. A surprise. The baker decorated it special. It's Snoopy kickin' a football. Keegan'll love it. I bet Coach Bryant'll like it too. Bottoms up!

(BRODY *and* MARY MERLE *drink.*)

MARY MERLE: At least stay till the storm clears.

BRODY: I'll leave the lantern.

MARY MERLE: You don't have to do that.

BRODY: I have others.

MARY MERLE: Another sip?

BRODY: I should be getting on.

MARY MERLE: I surely understand.

(*Awkward pause.*)

MARY MERLE: Look at us. Two old souls sitting in the dark together.

BRODY: Indeed.

MARY MERLE: Why, Mr Brody, I believe you've still got some dried blood coming out your nose.

BRODY: It's not blood.

MARY MERLE: What is it then?

BRODY: Red dirt.

MARY MERLE: Oh. (*Pause*) Well, you're too kind, for letting me keep the entire month's rent. You watch yourself out there. Seems that two-headed cow somehow got loose. No telling what it's capable of.

BRODY: I'll be careful.

MARY MERLE: Can you believe it, Mr Brody? My own boy's gunna be educated at the University of Alabama? I didn't think it possible. Did you know the Union army burned the school to the ground during the war? (*Genuinely hurt at the thought*) They set it aflame. And they didn't even have to. Such a grand institution. And for what? Just to be cruel. Just to be mean. And yet it's rebuilt, beaming brighter than ever. Up from the ashes, like the—the—

BRODY: The phoenix.

MARY MERLE: Like the phoenix. The mighty phoenix. Up from the ashes. Like the phoenix, and my boy, and this family, and the whole of the South.

BRODY: Yes.

MARY MERLE: I'm gibbering like an old biddy. Must be the drink. I know you need to get on.

BRODY: Be well, Mrs Moon.

MARY MERLE: Take care, Mr Brody.

(With a nod, BRODY exits.)

MARY MERLE: *(Calling at the stairs)* Posey! Get on down here! Your brother and Coach Bryant will be here any minute!

RUTHIE: *(Coming down the stairs)* Hey, Mother Moon! Sorry!

MARY MERLE: What're you doing up there?

RUTHIE: Oh, I was just returning Keegan's letterman jacket to his room.

MARY MERLE: You two kaput?

RUTHIE: Yes mam.

MARY MERLE: I figured he'd be movin' on.

RUTHIE: Oh?

MARY MERLE: You ain't good enough for him, girl. Especially now. What'd you do to your face?

KEEGAN: *(From outside)* Wooooooo-hoooooo!!!

MARY MERLE: That's him! He's here! Posey!

RUTHIE: I'm gunna slip out the side door.

MARY MERLE: You can't be going out in this storm.

RUTHIE: I can't be here. I can't see him.

MARY MERLE: You stay put!

KEEGAN: *(From outside)* Wooooooo-hoooooo!!!

MARY MERLE: Posey! Your brother's here!

(KEEGAN enters howling, strutting and pulsing with energy. RUTHIE shrinks into a corner of the room, as inconspicuous as possible.)

KEEGAN: Home, mama! Mama! I'm home!

MARY MERLE: My boy! My beautiful boy! *(She kisses him.)* Where's Coach Bryant?

KEEGAN: They decided to stop at the filling station before it closed. Wanted to be sure they had a full tank to drive back to Tuscaloosa tonight. They'll be here shortly.

MARY MERLE: *(Rushing up the stairs)* I'm gunna hunt some more candles upstairs. There's cake on the table.

KEEGAN: Cake! I'm starved!

MARY MERLE: Save a slice for Coach Bryant! Posey! You up here?

KEEGAN: *(Takes cake from box, searches for a knife to slice it; puts phone back on hook)* I'm so wired, mama! I just wanna keep kickin', y'know? Like a friggin' machine! Gimme anything and I'll kick it! Even this toaster I'd kick! What would you do if I punted our toaster, mama?

MARY MERLE: Eat some cake! I'll be right down!

KEEGAN: I'm just kiddin', mama! I ain't gunna punt the toaster! *(He's on the verge of slicing the cake; sees RUTHIE in the shadows.)* Who's that? Who's there?

RUTHIE: It's me.

KEEGAN: Ruthie? You weren't at the game.

RUTHIE: Naw.

KEEGAN: You missed some night.

RUTHIE: Bear Bryant come?

KEEGAN: Every bit of'im. And I showed him the goods. Best game of my life. Six kicks. All over fifty yards, the last one went for sixty-one.

RUTHIE: That's your record.

KEEGAN: By two yards. I's unstoppable.

RUTHIE: Rain held off?

KEEGAN: Till my last kick. Then the dangdest thing. It starts to pour like you never seen. Drops so thick they smart, poundin' like a billion men marchin'. It was as if I'd broke the sky with my last kick. As if it sailed so high it pricked the night and brought the rain. As if I made it rain. As if I's a god.

RUTHIE: He offered the scholarship?

KEEGAN: Bear Bryant? He's basically on his knees. Too bad you didn't play your cards, Ruthie. I coulda got you in on it. He'd have given anything to get me.

RUTHIE: You mention my name?

KEEGAN: Why would I done that?

RUTHIE: Can't all of us bring the rain.

KEEGAN: You're not wrong there.

RUTHIE: You're a stupid boy.

KEEGAN: For seeing things simple.

RUTHIE: For takin' pride in it.

KEEGAN: You sound like my brother.

RUTHIE: Do I? Good.

KEEGAN: Good?

RUTHIE: I think I love him.

KEEGAN: Who? Posey?

RUTHIE: I think I do.

KEEGAN: Love him! You barely know him!

RUTHIE: We been carryin' on right in front of you, if you had the sense to notice.

KEEGAN: What?

RUTHIE: You heard me.

KEEGAN: Posey?

RUTHIE: Yep.

KEEGAN: My own brother! My own faggot brother!

RUTHIE: Jealous?

KEEGAN: Ha! Ain't that wild! I made it rain!

RUTHIE: I think you are. I think he frightens you.

KEEGAN: Oh please.

RUTHIE: I know what you stole from him.

KEEGAN: You don't know nothin'.

RUTHIE: Firsthand, I seen what he's got left. His one and only. I've seen it, Keegan. I've held it.

(As KEEGAN *seethes,* MARY MERLE *reenters, bubbly, holding candles.)*

MARY MERLE: Found them! I knew I had some scented ones. They'll add some fragrance to the festivities! Keegan, you ain't even touched your Snoopy cake. Look, he's kickin' a football! Ain't it a gas!

KEEGAN: I lost my appetite.

MARY MERLE: Somethin' wrong?

(The phone rings. KEEGAN *answers, trying to defuse his rage.)*

KEEGAN: *(On phone)* Hello! Yes, this is him! What? This a joke? You're kidding. Oh, that's bad. Well, what'd he say? He does? Yeah. Uh-huh. I understand. No no, I do. Bye. *(Hangs up phone.)*

MARY MERLE: What is it?

KEEGAN: Coach Bryant's car collided with the two-headed cow.

MARY MERLE: Oh Jesus.

KEEGAN: He's dead.

MARY MERLE: Oh Jesus!

KEEGAN: The cow.

MARY MERLE: I thought you was talking about Coach Bryant!

KEEGAN: Coach Bryant's just scratched up. Totaled his car. Coach Tutt says he's gunna give him a lift back to Tuscaloosa. Says Coach Bryant ain't in much of visiting mood, but the scholarship offer still stands.

MARY MERLE: That poor man.

RUTHIE: I wonder if the cow suffered much.

KEEGAN: Apparently there's bits of it all over the road.

MARY MERLE: Well, that's that then.

RUTHIE: I'll go tell Posey.

MARY MERLE: You stay there, girl.

KEEGAN: I wanted to show the Bear my home.

MARY MERLE: I know you did, honey.

KEEGAN: I coulda shown him my trophies, and my weights, and daddy's gun collection.

MARY MERLE: He'll see it another time.

(KEEGAN, *glancing at the guns on the wall, notices something amiss.*)

RUTHIE: Posey really ought to know Bear Bryant ain't comin'.

KEEGAN: You stay put.

MARY MERLE: What's your hurry, girl?

KEEGAN: There's a gun missing.

MARY MERLE: Huh?

KEEGAN: From the wall. A gun's missing. Look. (*Indicating the Colt's empty slot*) There!

MARY MERLE: Sure 'nough!

KEEGAN: Where's he at?

MARY MERLE: Who?

KEEGAN: That—man!

MARY MERLE: Brody?

KEEGAN: Yeah!

MARY MERLE: He's gone. He left.

KEEGAN: My god, mama, you see what you done?

MARY MERLE: You think—?

KEEGAN: He took it! He stole one of daddy's gun!

MARY MERLE: Oh, I don't know if—

KEEGAN: It's plain as day, mama! This is what happens when you let one of'em in! They're not like us! Get the sheriff on the phone! I'm going after him!

MARY MERLE: I had no idea he'd do this.

RUTHIE: He didn't.

KEEGAN: You shut up!

MARY MERLE: He seemed so polite.

KEEGAN: You can't trust'em! They got no respect for property, for tradition!

MARY MERLE: I was so stupid.

KEEGAN: When did he leave?

MARY MERLE: A few minutes ago.

KEEGAN: I'll catch him.

MARY MERLE: In this storm?

KEEGAN: And when I do, I'll—

(POSEY *has entered and is standing at the bottom of the stairs.*)

POSEY: Give it a rest.

KEEGAN: This don't mind you.

POSEY: *(Holding up the gun)* It don't?

MARY MERLE: Posey's got the gun!

KEEGAN: *(Snatching the gun away from him)* Gimme that!

MARY MERLE: Posey, you know you're not to touch the collection.

KEEGAN: He was up to somethin', I can tell.

MARY MERLE: You gave us such scare.

KEEGAN: What was you doin' with it?

POSEY: It don't work.

KEEGAN: 'Course it works. It ain't even been fired.

POSEY: It jammed up.

KEEGAN: Guns like this don't jam!

MARY MERLE: Keegan, you told your brother the good news?

KEEGAN: Like he matters.

MARY MERLE: He got the scholarship, Posey.

POSEY: Just as well.

MARY MERLE: You gunna congratulate your brother?

POSEY: Me and Ruthie—we're leavin'.

MARY MERLE: What?

POSEY: We're taking daddy's old pickup, and we're not coming back.

MARY MERLE: You can't go. You're just kids. Who do you think—?

POSEY: Bye, mama.

MARY MERLE: But where?

POSEY: Just not here.

MARY MERLE: You'll be back by mornin', you damn fools.

(POSEY *and* RUTHIE *are at the front door.*)

KEEGAN: *(Preoccupied with the gun)* Hey, fruit, how do you know the gun don't fire?

POSEY: I tried to use it.

KEEGAN: How?

POSEY: The two-headed cow.

MARY MERLE: It was you who set it free.

POSEY: I found its cage at the fair. In the rain, under a blue tarp. I slipped under, and there he was, two-headed and starin' back, not five inches from my face. Contemplatin' me, like he'd known me. As if he was expectin' me. All that longin' and sufferin'. And I understood just what to do. I pressed the gun to one of its noses, pulled the trigger, but it jams, see. And the cow just glares at me, pleadin' somehow. I couldn't leave it that way. And so I opened its cage. And I left him.

KEEGAN: A lot of good that did it. Bear Bryant done pulverized it in his Buick.

RUTHIE: Let's go.

POSEY: Be sure to feed the dogs.

KEEGAN: First we finish this thing.

POSEY: It's done.

KEEGAN: Your stupid stunt is the reason I ain't sittin' with Coach Bryant right now.

POSEY: I said it's done.

KEEGAN: No sir, it ain't done.

(POSEY *and* RUTHIE *begin to head out the front door.*)

KEEGAN: Hey! Don't you walk away from me! (*Pointing the gun.*) I'll shoot! I swear to god!

POSEY: Gun don't work, Keegan.

KEEGAN: Like I'm gunna believe you?

POSEY: It's been sittin' up on the wall too long. See for yourself. Fire away!

KEEGAN: Maybe I will!

RUTHIE: Come on, Posey!

POSEY: So long.

(POSEY *and* RUTHIE *exit.*)

KEEGAN: (*Moving to the door*) Wait! I *will* fire! I ain't afraid! I'll call your bluff! Come back! Both of ya! I'll fire!

(KEEGAN, *realizing they have no intention of stopping, moves from the door back into the house. He begins to inspect the gun, turning it over in his hands and checking the barrel.*)

MARY MERLE: Keegan, maybe you'd ought to put the gun back on its rack.

KEEGAN: Don't work...what do they know! Stupid queer probably forgot to cock it—

(The gun discharges, blowing a bullet through KEEGAN'S *foot. He drops quickly, screaming in pain. There's blood.* MARY MERLE *rushes to him.)*

MARY MERLE: Keegan!

KEEGAN: AHHHHHHHH!!!!

MARY MERLE: No! No!

KEEGAN: AHHHHHHHH!!!!

MARY MERLE: Baby boy! Baby boy!

KEEGAN: I shot off my foot, mama!

MARY MERLE: My lord!

KEEGAN: My kickin' foot! Oh my god, mama!

MARY MERLE: We'll get you to the hospital!

KEEGAN: I shot off my foot, mama!

MARY MERLE: We'll take the station wagon!

(In the pandemonium of the moment, she lifts KEEGAN *the best she can and they begin to make their way out the front door.)*

KEEGAN: Mama! Oh, mama!

MARY MERLE: It's gunna be alright, baby boy!

KEEGAN: *(Weirdly, a sense of validation)* I knew it'd work, mama! Posey was wrong! See, it did fire! It did work!

MARY MERLE: Yes, baby boy, it did work!

KEEGAN: After all these years!

*(*KEEGAN *and* MARY MERLE *exit out the front door. We hear* KEEGAN *wailing with pain and car doors opening and closing. After a moment,* MARY MERLE *rushes back in.)*

MARY MERLE: *(Searching the house frantically)* Keys! Keys! Where's my car keys! Where are they! *(After several seconds of searching, she realizes they are in her pocket.)* My pocket. In my pocket the whole time.

(MARY MERLE *laughs lightly, despairingly at this. The laugh turns into weeping, then great sobbing. As she sobs, beams of light and engine-like rumblings happen above the Moon home, just as we saw before. The house shakes. Cups, saucers, picture frames, and the like, begin to fall from rattling furniture and shelves. Abruptly, the rumbling and trembling stop, though the beams of light still shine through. In the brightness, she sobs on. This is all that is heard.*)

(*Blackout*)

END OF PLAY